FARM TRACTORS

Andrew Morland

OLIVER
ROW CROP 77

MBI

First published in 1993 by MBI, an imprint of
MBI Publishing Company, Galtier Plaza, Suite 200,
380 Jackson Street, St. Paul, MN 55101-3885 USA

MBI titles are also available at discounts in bulk
quantity for industrial or sales-promotional use. For
details write to Special Sales Manager at Motorbooks
International Wholesalers & Distributors, Galtier
Plaza, Suite 200, 380 Jackson Street, St. Paul, MN
55101-3885 USA.

ISBN 0-7603-2025-X

Edited by Heather Oakley and Steve Gansen
Designed by Kou Lor

Front cover: **1938 Graham-Bradley**
This 32-horsepower tractor was powered by the six-cylinder Graham Paige engine with a 3.25x4.75 inch bore and stroke. This long-stroke engine gave a 20-mile-per-hour top speed. Car builder Graham-Paige Motors Corporation of Detroit, Michigan, produced this row-crop model in 1938, followed by the 104 model in 1939. This was the same tractor but had standard tread. Production ceased in 1945.

Frontis: **Duplex Co-op No. 2**
The top-of-the-range Co-op No. 2 was powered by the smooth, powerful six-cylinder Chrysler engine, which gave a reputed top speed of 28 miles per hour. This rare tractor is owned by Ivan Henderson of Hutchinson, Ontario, Canada.

Title page: **Oliver Row Crop 77**
In 1948, Oliver introduced its Fleetline Series of tractors with modern styling and streamlined, enclosed engines. The Row Crop 66, 77, and 88 models replaced the old 60, 70, and 80 models, respectively, and were built until 1954. This powerful, smooth, six-cylinder, 40-horsepower Row Crop 77 was typical of the new fleetlines, and boasted the new Hydra-Lectric hydraulics system beginning in 1949.

Back cover: **Minneapolis-Moline UDLX**
The UDLX Comfortractor was some 30 years ahead of its time, and many farmers chose the more-traditional, open-cab Model U tractor over the UDLX. Because of its avant-garde design and high cost of $2,155, only about 150 were sold during its production run from 1938 to 1941. This 1938 UDLX is part of the Roger Mohr collection.

Printed in China

Contents

Acknowledgments

Thank you to all the enthusiastic owners of classic farm tractors in America and Canada, whose help and cooperation made this book possible.

Special thanks to the following for allowing me to take photographs on their sites: Roger Mohr Collection, Vail, Iowa; The Two-Cylinder Club and the John Deere Historic Site at Grand Detour, Dixon, Illinois; and the Ontario Agricultural Museum, Milton, Canada. Thanks also to the Keller family of Forest Junction, Wisconsin, for allowing me to photograph their rare John Deere tractors.

For information on tractor events in the United States and Canada, I recommend the Steam and Gas Show Directory, printed annually by Stemgas Publishing Company, PO Box 328, Lancaster Pennsylvania 17603.

Chapter 1

International Harvester Tractors
The International Red Farmall Farms All

In 1906, the International Harvester Company of Chicago created its first tractor, which eventually evolved into the famous Farmall.

The Farmall became the quintessential tractor, the one by which all others were judged. It was designed with the small-scale farmer in mind and brought "power farming" within the reach of farmers throughout the United States and Canada, due to its small size and low price.

The roots of the International Harvester Company stretch back to the mid-1800s when Cyrus Hall McCormick created his first reaper. McCormick's chief competition in the field came from the Deering family, but with tough times in the farming marketplace, the Deerings offered a merger. On August 12, 1902, the International Harvester Company (IH) was born.

Alongside its Farmall tractor, IH offered a broad range of farm machinery from threshers to combines to discs to plows. In the late 1970s, the United Automobile Workers (UAW) struck IH and, along with the depressed farm economy, forced International to cut back. In the mid-1980s, IH was acquired by Tenneco, which also owned Case.

ON PAGE 8: 1940 FARMALL M

The large four-cylinder 247.7-ci gasoline-engine tractor was the replacement for the F30 and was rated at 36 horsepower at PTO and 24.5 horsepower at the drawbar. Owner—John Poch.

ABOVE: 1929 INTERNATIONAL FARMALL REGULAR

This was the first row-crop tractor with dual-narrow front wheels and a steering rod over the top of the engine. The Farmall Regular, introduced in 1924 and followed by the F-12, F-14, F-20 and F-30, kept the same design until the lettered series appeared in 1939. These were styled by Raymond Loewy, with modern panels covering the same Regular concept. The Regular has a three-speed transmission with a four-cylinder engine rated at 18 horsepower. Owners—John & Mary Lou Poch of New Holstein, Wisconsin.

RIGHT: MCCORMICK-DEERING W-30

The International Harvester Company built more than 32,000 W30s from 1932 to 1940. The gasoline/kerosene engine put out 19.7 horsepower at the drawbar and 31.2 horsepower at the belt. W-30s had a 3-speed gearbox until 1938. After that, a 4-speed was standard. The engine hood's side door has been removed to show the tall, long-stroke four-cylinder engine that was developed from the 15-30 model. Note the two hand-hole covers in the engine block for easy access. Photographed on the Kurt Umnus Farm, Edgar, Wisconsin, during the North Central Steam and Gas Engine Show.

ABOVE: INTERNATIONAL HARVESTER MCCORMICK W-4
The W-4 was introduced in 1940 and continued production until 1953. Designed as a standard-tread version of the Farmall H model, it also shared the H four-cylinder, 152ci C-152 engine. The W-4 was designed with a cast-iron frame, five-speed gearbox, and independent braking system. The engine was rated at a full 24 horsepower. This W-4 was photographed in Great Britain, where many W-4s, W-6s, and W-9s arrived under the World War II lend-lease agreements with the United States.

RIGHT: INTERNATIONAL 1941 FARMALL B
The four-cylinder 113.1-ci gasoline engine with 6:1 compression ratio was rated at 16.8 horsepower. A lower 5:1 compression ratio was available with the kerosene version rated at 16.5 horsepower.

ABOVE: INTERNATIONAL FARMALL SUPER M

The gas-powered Super M was built from 1952 to 1953 and featured an adjustable tread width that could be stretched from 52 to 88 inches. This superbly restored example is owned by the Bunker family of Lena, Illinois.

13

INTERNATIONAL HARVESTER FARMALL 300

The Farmall 300 model was introduced in 1954 as a three-plow, general-purpose row-crop tractor. It was powered by International Harvester's four-cylinder C-169 engine with a bore and stroke that measured 3.56x4.25 inches. The 300s short life ended in 1956 after only two years of production.

14

RIGHT: INTERNATIONAL FARMALL 300

Built in 1956 with a dual-narrow front end, this three-plow, 40-horsepower gasoline tractor of 169-ci displacement weighed over 5,000 pounds. The 300 was also available with an LPG engine, but no diesel version was offered. The later 350 was offered with the 193-ci diesel engine built by Continental.

BELOW: INTERNATIONAL 450 DIESEL

The Farmall 450 was built from 1956 to 1958 in gasoline, LPG, and diesel versions. The 281-ci diesel is a powerful four-bottom plow tractor. Nearly 40,000 Farmall 450s were sold worldwide.

Chapter 2

John Deere Tractors
The Waterloo Boy and Deere Green Poppin' Johnny

Deere and Company has grown from a small, one-man blacksmith shop making steel plows to a giant international corporation. Along the way, Deere and Company have built everything from automobiles to snowmobiles to bicycles to airplanes. But it is the John Deere farm tractor, and its accompanying line of implements, that have made Deere the world's most famous agricultural equipment manufacturer.

Deere's entry into the tractor field was belated when compared with other American farm equipment makers. Deere was concentrating on the production of its plows and other select implements at the turn of the century and was not ready to get into the power-farming field.

Deere began experimenting with Melvin, Dain, and Sklovsky tractors in the 1910s before purchasing the Waterloo Gasoline Engine Company of Waterloo, Iowa, in 1918. Waterloo built its own tractor, the Waterloo Boy, which was then added to the John Deere line.

When the Waterloo Boy became outdated, Deere developed its own tractor based largely on the Waterloo Boy. The Model D made its debut in 1924, followed by the famous line of two-cylinder, general-purpose row-crop tractors. From 1934 to 1960, these "Poppin' Johnnies" built the Deere legend.

ON PAGE 16: JOHN DEERE MODEL BWH

After creating the Model D as a replacement for the Waterloo Boy, Deere engineers turned their hands to designing a general-purpose tractor that small farmers could afford to own and operate. After building several experimental prototypes, Deere released a limited run of its new row-crop tractor, the Model C, which was soon refined and renamed the GP, for general-purpose. The Model B replaced the GP in 1935 and was powered by a two-cylinder 149-ci engine with a bore and stroke of 4.25x5.25 inches backed by a four-speed gearbox. The BWH was a Model B Hi-Crop variation with an adjustable, wide-tread front axle. This very collectible unstyled Deere is owned by the Keller family of Forest Junction, Wisconsin.

ABOVE: WATERLOO BOY MODEL R

The Waterloo Gasoline Engine Company of Waterloo, Iowa, built the Waterloo Boy tractor, which garnered such a strong reputation that Deere and Company bought out the whole company. The Model R was built from 1914 to 1919. The 465-ci two-cylinder engine had a bore and stroke measuring 6.50x7.00 inches and was rated at 16 horsepower at the drawbar. The owner of this beautifully restored Model R is Tony Ridgeway of West Unity, Ohio.

LEFT: WATERLOO BOY MODEL R

Detail of the gorgeous Waterloo Boy emblem that highlights the fuel tank of the Model R.

In 1960, Deere introduced its new line of modern three-, four-, and six-cylinder tractors, still painted in the famous Deere Green with yellow trim. Deere continued into the 1990s with a full line of two- and four-wheel-drive tractors, combines, and implements.

JOHN DEERE MODEL A

The year 1934 witnessed the debut of John Deere's new general-purpose row-crop models, including the Model A. This 1934 A featured an open fan shaft, which can be seen rotating on the engine. The owner of this early A is Jim Quinn of East Peoria, Illinois.

ABOVE: JOHN DEERE MODEL A

The Model A was a general-purpose row-crop tractor built from 1934 to 1952. It was designed to fill in the John Deere line between the one-plow Model GP and the three-plow Model D; thus, the Model A could pull two plows. This early, unstyled A was powered by Deere's famous two-cylinder 309-ci engine, rated at 16.22 drawbar horsepower and 23.523 belt horsepower at the University of Nebraska Tractor Tests. More than 300,000 units were built during its production run in several variations that included the AN single front-wheel model; AW adjustable-axle, wide front model; ANH and AWH Hi-Crop versions; AR standard-tread, non-row-crop model; AO orchard tractor; and streamlined AOS. This A is owned by the Keller family of Forest Junction, Wisconsin.

RIGHT: JOHN DEERE MODEL B

The Model B was the quintessential Poppin' Johnny two-cylinder, general-purpose row-crop John Deere tractor. Introduced in 1935, this particular tractor is serial number B1000, the very first Model B produced. In all, more than 300,000 Model Bs were sold, marking it John Deere's best-selling tractor. This historic Model B belongs to the Keller family of Forest Junction, Wisconsin.

NEXT PAGE: JOHN DEERE AW WIDE TREAD

The unstyled AW was built in 1935 and featured French and Hecht spoked wheels. The two-cylinder gasoline engine was rated at 34 horsepower. The kerosene Model A Row Crop was rated at 26 horsepower.

RIGHT: JOHN DEERE MODEL 70

The Model 70 arrived in 1953 as the Model G successor, designed as a tough, strong tractor that was born to pull. This 70 featured a diesel engine backed with power steering. The two-cylinder diesel produced 45.7 drawbar horsepower from its 376-ci. A V-4–cylinder gasoline pony engine of 18.8-ci was used as a starter for Deere's first diesel row-crop tractor. Production of the Model 70 series lasted from 1953 to 1956, when it was replaced by the new Model 720 series. This 70 is owned by Richard Rammanger of Morrisonville, Wisconsin.

FAR RIGHT: JOHN DEERE MODEL 70 HI-CROP

The Model 70 was the replacement for the illustrious Model G, John Deere's three-plow general-purpose tractor. This Hi-Crop version of the 70 now stood in for the old GH Hi-Crop. This 70 featured power steering and the engine could run on LP gas. The 379.5-ci two-cylinder LPG was rated at 46.1 horsepower at the drawbar. Built from 1953 to 1956, it came with six forward gears and one reverse. This very collectible 70 was one of only twenty-five built, and is owned by Norman Smith of Carrollton, Illinois.

BELOW: JOHN DEERE STYLED MODEL A

This 1948 Model A powers a Ross Junior baler of the same year. The Ransomes Simms & Jefferies thresher is in the background. Photographs taken at the Great Dorset Steam Fair, Blandford Forum, Great Britain.

JOHN DEERE MODEL 60 ROW CROP

The Model 60 Series replaced the grand old Model A in 1952. Its two-cylinder engine of 321ci was rated at 36.9 horsepower at the drawbar. The Model 60 was built until 1956, when the Model 620 took its place. This Model 60 is owned by Richard Rammanger of Morrisonville, Wisconsin.

JOHN DEERE MODEL 320

The Model 320 arrived in the nation's fields in 1956 as a new model derived from the original Models H and M. The 320 was designed especially for the small farmer and vegetable grower and came in two versions, the 320S, or Standard, and the 320U, or Utility. The 320 was powered by a two-cylinder, 22.4-horsepower gasoline engine of 100.5 ci. This 320 was photographed at the Two-Cylinder Club's show at the John Deere Historic Site in Grand Detour, Dixon, Illinois.

ABOVE: 1964 JOHN DEERE 5010 DIESEL

The largest of the New Generation of John Deere, the 5010 was manufactured from 1962 to 1965. Sold as a 117-horsepower diesel by John Deere, the 531cc engine was tested at Nebraska and proved to have 121.1 brake horsepower and 108.9 horsepower at the drawbar.

LEFT: JOHN DEERE 830

The 1959 830 had a two-cylinder 70-horsepower diesel engine and a V-4 gasoline starter motor. The 830 was produced from 1958 to 1960 with nearly 6,900 sold. The 830 was the replacement for the 820 with the 472-ci two-cylinder engine. The ultimate two-cylinder John Deere was big, very heavy, and costly to run. The 830 is very collectible today as the top of the range and the last of its type.

Chapter 3

J. I. Case Tractors
The Old Abe Mascot and Flambeau Red Tractors

Jerome Increase Case founded his J. I. Case Threshing Machine Company in Rochester, Wisconsin, in 1843. The firm's first creation was a groundhog-type thresher; within a short time Case graduated to building steam engine–powered traction engines that were mammoth in size and power. In 1847, Case moved his firm to Racine, Wisconsin.

In 1876, Case started a separate company with no ties to the threshing machine maker. This second firm, J. I. Case Plow Works, was founded in Racine to offer plows; it was eventually controlled by the Wallis Tractor Company before being sold to the Canadian Massey-Harris firm in the 1920s. In 1928, Massey sold the rights to the Case name back to J.I. Threshing Machine Company.

Production of gasoline-powered tractors at the threshing machine firm started in the 1910s as the demand for steam declined. The Model 30-60, 20-40, 12-45, and the four-cylinder 10-20 were offered beginning in 1912. In 1916, Case developed its Crossmotor models before moving on to standard and row-crop tractors in 1929. In the late 1930s, Case started painting its tractors the telltale Flambeau Red color.

In the late 1960s, Case was taken over by Tenneco, which continued to manufacture Case and International Harvester tractors in the 1990s.

ON PAGE 30: CASE STANDARD TREAD MODEL D
This Model D, built in 1950, has a Case Centennial 2x14-inch bottom plow. The four-cylinder overhead-valve gasoline engine was rated at 38 horsepower. Owner—Tom Graverson, Indiana.

ABOVE: CASE CROSSMOTOR 15-27
Close-up of the clutch and magneto on the Crossmotor. The hand-operated, twin-disc clutch was fitted inside the belt pulley. Case did not change to foot-operated clutches until 1955.

LEFT: CASE CROSSMOTOR 15-27
The J. I. Case Crossmotor 15-27 was first offered in 1919 with production continuing through 1924. It produced 27 horsepower at the belt and 15 horsepower at the drawbar. At a maximum engine speed of 900 rpm, 33 horsepower was available giving a top speed of 3 miles per hour. The four-cylinder 381-ci engine had a bore and stroke of 4.50x6.00 inches. At 6,350 pounds, the 15-27 was no lightweight. This 15-27 was photographed in the early morning sun with its correct LC Gray color and Case Red pinstripes. It is owned by Bill Kuhn of Kinde, Michigan.

CASE CROSSMOTOR 10-18

In the mid-1910s, tractor manufacturers began to focus on building tractors designed to handle two-, three-, and four-bottom plows. In 1916, J. I. Case introduced its Crossmotor Model 9-18, a lightweight, streamlined, two-plow tractor. In 1918 and 1919, Case boosted the 9-18's horsepower output by increasing engine rpm and redesignated it the Model 10-18. The 10-18 was tested at the University of Nebraska in April 1920, where its engine developed 18.41 belt horsepower and 11.24 drawbar horsepower. Maximum drawbar pull was measured at 1,730 pounds. A new feature of the 10-18 was Case's patented Air Washer, which drew outside air into a canister then through water that trapped dirt particles. A screen then filtered out the dust and clean air continued through the system into the carburetor. The 10-18 was offered in both agricultural and industrial models. This 1919 Crossmotor 10-18 was photographed with owner and restorer John Davis of Maplewood, Ohio, at the controls.

LEFT: CASE R

This Case R, built in 1938, was powered by the L-head, four-cylinder Waukesha engine with a 3.25x4.00 inch bore and stroke. Rated at 14 horsepower at the drawbar and 18 horsepower at the belt, the R Series led the way for Case until World War II. This R is owned by Betty and Lee Norton of Alto, Michigan.

NEXT PAGE:
1942 CASE SC ROW CROP

A two-plow tractor, the S series used a modern, shorter-stroke, high-speed engine with a rated speed of 1,550 rpm. At the Nebraska Tests, running on distillate, a maximum PTO horsepower of 16.18 was achieved. Near the end of production in 1953 the engine was bored out and the S almost became a 30-horsepower tractor on gasoline. The Flambeau Red S production ran from 1941 to 1954.

ABOVE: **CASE VAH HIGH CLEARANCE**

The High Clearance model was built in 1953 for cane production with adjustable front and rear tread, narrow and wide axle. From 1948 the VA models used the Case Eagle Hitch system of hitch but no draft control because Ferguson had the rights. Continental Motors built the VA four-cylinder, overhead-valve engine originally, but in 1947 Case took over production. The VA was produced from 1942 to 1955.

LEFT: **CASE DCS**

The Sugar Cane Special of 1952 is very rare and collectible today by virtue of its limited production. The DC has a four-cylinder engine with 32.94 belt horsepower and 25.74 horsepower at the drawbar, with a bore and stroke of 3.875x5.500 inches.

Chapter 4

Minneapolis-Moline Tractors
The Prairie Gold Minne-Mo

The history of American farm equipment manufacturers is a history of corporate mergers. Firms struggled to stay alive in the fast-growing and rapidly changing marketplace after the turn of the century, and one way to build a strong company with a complete line of farming tools was to merge several firms into one.

Minneapolis-Moline Company (MM) of Minneapolis, Minnesota, was formed in 1929 by the merger of Minneapolis Steel & Machinery Company of Minneapolis; the Moline Implement Company of Moline, Illinois; and the Minneapolis Threshing Machine Company of Hopkins, Minnesota.

With this combined force, the new company was able to offer farmers a full line of equipment including the famous Twin City tractors, Minneapolis threshers, and a variety of implements, grain drills, wagons, and tillage tools.

"Minne-Mo" became one of the stalwart American tractor manufacturers of the 1930s and postwar years. Its Prairie Gold–painted tractors were easily identified against the green of fields, and farmers came to rely on the power and dependability of the tractors and equipment.

Minneapolis-Moline became part of White Farm Equipment in 1963, joining Oliver and Cockshutt. In 1972, production was transferred from Minneapolis, Minnesota, to Charles City, Iowa. The MM name was dropped from tractors in 1974 and replaced by the White name.

ON PAGE 40: 1948 MINNEAPOLIS-MOLINE UTC CANE
This exceptionally high-crop tractor, with high-arch front axle, was specifically designed for the cane crop. The overhead-valve gasoline four-cylinder engine has a 4.5x5.0 inch bore and stroke.

RIGHT: MINNEAPOLIS-MOLINE UDLX
The UDLX Comfortractor was some 30 years ahead of its time, and many farmers chose the more-traditional, open-cab Model U tractor over the UDLX. Because of its avant-garde design and high cost of $2,155, only about 150 were sold during its production run from 1938 to 1941. This 1938 UDLX is part of the Roger Mohr collection.

LEFT: MINNEAPOLIS-MOLINE UDLX

The Comfortractor shared its engine with the Model U. With 40 to 45 horsepower on tap, top speed was 40 miles per hour. With its easy-change five-speed gearbox and foot throttle, the UDLX was designed to plow all day then be driven downtown in the evening—a combination car and tractor for the modern farmer of the 1930s!

ABOVE: MINNEAPOLIS-MOLINE UDLX

The Comfortractor was designed with safety and weather protection in mind. The insulated, impact-resistant cab featured safety glass, windshield wipers, radio, heater, and hot-air defrosting—all the comforts of a car. As with many advanced designs, the UDLX attracted few customers in its day. Today, it is one of the most collectible MMs.

MINNEAPOLIS-MOLINE GTA

This 1946 GTA was designed to pull a four- to five-plow load. The engine was a four-cylinder 403.2 ci with paired blocks. The bore and stroke measured 4.625x6.000 inches. Backed by a four-speed gearbox and rated at 49 horsepower, the engine produced a maximum belt power of 55 horsepower. All engines came standard with force-fed lubrication and a balanced camshaft for smooth running. This massive engine alone weighs more than one ton. The GTA sported a yellow grille whereas the early GT had a red grille. This GTA is from the Roger Mohr collection.

ABOVE: 1947 MINNEAPOLIS-MOLINE GTA LPG
The liquid propane gas GTA has the four-cylinder MM
engine with two paired blocks. Owner—Ernest Weissert.

RIGHT: MINNEAPOLIS-MOLINE RTU
The four-cylinder engine of the 1949 RTU was rated at 20 to
24 horsepower at 1,400 rpm. The engine had a 3.625x4.000
inch bore and stroke with unusually long rocker arms and
horizontal valves. Only two main bearings held the
crankshaft, but the front was an extra-strong roller bearing.
Overall, the engine design was a great success, offering ease
of maintenance and a long life. The owner of this RTU is Jim
Adams of Marshalltown, Iowa.

ABOVE: 1957 MINNEAPOLIS-MOLINE 335 UTILITY

The 335 was manufactured from 1956 to 1961. The four-cylinder overhead-valve gasoline engine was rated at 29.87 belt horsepower. The Ampli-Torc, a torque-amplifier system between the clutch and gearbox, gave the equivalent of 10 forward speeds from the standard five-speed gearbox.

LEFT: MINNEAPOLIS-MOLINE BF AVERY

In 1951 Minneapolis-Moline took over Avery tractors of Louisville, Kentucky, and produced the Model V, a Hercules-engined Avery in Minneapolis-Moline colors, until 1955.

BELOW: MINNEAPOLIS-MOLINE M5

By the 1960s, Minneapolis-Moline production was centered at White Farm Equipment's Hopkins, Minnesota, plant. This M5 tractor from 1960 was typical of the new generation of White-built MMs. The four-cylinder engine had a bore and stroke of 4.625x5.000 inches. Power steering was standard. This M5 is from the Roger Mohr collection.

Chapter 5

Massey Tractors
The Pride of Canada

The Massey-Harris Company was the result of a merger in 1891 of two stalwart Ontario, Canada, agricultural firms—Massey Manufacturing Company of Toronto and A. Harris, Son & Company of Brantford.

Massey-Harris made its debut in the tractor market in 1917 with the Bull tractor, built by the Bull Tractor Company of Minneapolis, Minnesota, which later became the Toro Company. By 1918, Massey-Harris was building its own tractor, the MH-1, based on a design by the Parret Tractor Company of Chicago.

Massey-Harris continued to build a wide range of row-crop, general-purpose tractors but the firm's product was refined in the mid-1950s when it merged with Harry Ferguson, Inc. Ferguson had developed the three-point hitch and draft control that revolutionized Henry Ford's N Series of tractors; with this merger, Massey Ferguson was formed and a new line of models was created.

ON PAGE 48: MASSEY-HARRIS PONY

Built in 1949, at the Woodstock factory in Canada, the Pony was Massey-Harris' smallest model. The 62-ci Continental four-cylinder engine had a bore and stroke of 2.375x3.500 inches. The Pony was rated as a 10-horsepower or one-plow tractor. This Pony is owned by Bill Kuhn of Kinde, Michigan.

LEFT: MASSEY-HARRIS 81 R

Massey-Harris built its 81 R standard-tread tractor from 1941 to 1946, during which time it was used extensively by the Royal Canadian Air Force. In 1946 production switched to row-crop style 81 Rs, which continued to 1948. This 81 R was built in 1942 and bears serial number 425727. This tractor is owned by Diane Fisher of Milton, Ontario.

ABOVE: MASSEY-HARRIS NO. 3

The No. 3 was a refinement of the Parrett-designed No. 2.
Despite repositioning the radiator to update the look, the
No. 3 still had a strange stance. The front axle had to
remain far forward to retain the steering lock required
by the large-diameter front wheels. The refined No. 3
was rated at 15 to 28 horsepower.

RIGHT: MASSEY-HARRIS NO. 3

The horsepower increase to 28 on the belt at 1,000 rpm was
derived from the enlarged Massey-Harris No. 2 Buda engine.
Bore and stroke was now at 4.50x6.50 inches. But even the
power increase failed to sell the tractor in the highly-
competitive agricultural market. In 1923, the year this
tractor was built, production stopped at the Weston factory.
This No. 3 is owned by the Ontario Agricultural Museum.

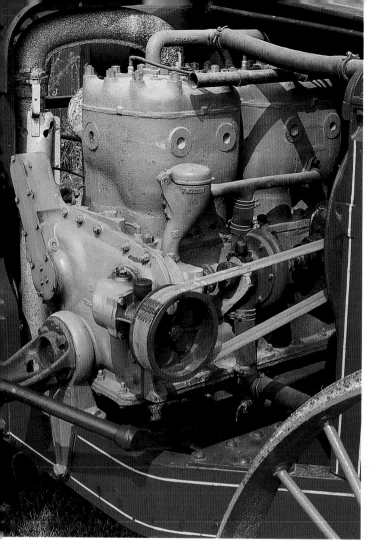

ABOVE: MASSEY-HARRIS MODEL NO. 3

The four-cylinder Buda engine was mounted transversely in the No. 3s frame. The fan belt drive turned 90 degrees to run the oil and magneto shaft and allow for easy access. Crank starting was on the right side of the engine with pulley power take-off on the other side.

RIGHT: MASSEY-HARRIS 102GS JUNIOR TWIN-POWER

The 102 Series tractors were popular in the late 1930s and 1940s. This 102GS Junior had the added benefit of Twin-Power, which offered a range of different governor settings over the standard Junior. Built in 1945, this 102GS boasted 25 horsepower. This tractor is owned by Ivan Henderson of Cambridge, Ontario.

MASSEY-HARRIS 101 SUPER ROW CROP

The 101 Super Row Crop was one of the most advanced and stylish Massey-Harris tractors. The streamlined bodywork completely enclosed the engine—an advanced design for its time. Today, the 101 Super with the Chrysler 35-horsepower, six-cylinder engine is probably the most collectible of the Massey-Harris range of tractors. Many 101 Supers lost their pretty, vented side panels around the farm or in the fields, however. The later 1940 to 1944 Supers had more conventional half-enclosed panels and Continental 26 to 40 horsepower side-valve engines. This 101 was built in 1939.

Chapter 6

Allis-Chalmers Tractors
The Persian Orange Tractors

Corporate mergers have always shaped the farm tractor and equipment industry, but the Allis-Chalmers Company stands ahead of all other manufacturers in the number of disparate companies that have joined together over the decades to form a single firm.

Allis-Chalmers' roots stretch back to 1847 when James Decker and Charles Seville formed a company to build flour-making tools; Edward P. Allis, one half of the Allis-Chalmers name, soon bought them out. In 1901, Allis joined with Fraser & Chalmers of Chicago, Dickson Manufacturing Company of Pennsylvania, and Gates Iron Works of Chicago to create Allis-Chalmers.

Allis built steam engines as early as 1869, but the new company's first tractors were unveiled after the turn of the century. Allis-Chalmers continued to add other companies to its corporate roster, including tractor builders such as the famous and long-lived Advance-Rumely Thresher Company and the Monarch Tractor Corporation, which constructed crawlers.

ON PAGE 56: ALLIS-CHALMERS D10
Built from 1959 to 1967, this model was the same as the D12, except that the D12 had larger rear axle sleeves and a wider front axle. The two-plow D10 tractor started life with the 139-ci four-cylinder Allis gasoline engine, but in 1961, starting from serial number 3501, the engine was enlarged to 149-ci displacement.

RIGHT: ALLIS-CHALMERS WD45 DIESEL
Built in 1955, the WD had the Buda diesel engine produced by the Buda Company of Harvey, Illinois. The six-cylinder 230-ci engine produced 43 belt horsepower. The WD 45 has the Allis Snap Coupler that allows genuine in-seat hitching. Owner—David Buttjer.

ABOVE: ALLIS-CHALMERS MODEL U
The Model U was one of Allis-Chalmers' best-selling tractor lines. Introduced in 1929, the Model U continued in production until 1952, by which time more than 20,000 units had been built. This U was manufactured in 1936. The four-cylinder Allis-Chalmers engine had a bore and stroke of 4.375x5.000 inches. This engine produced 33.18 horsepower at the drawbar at 1,200 rpm during the University of Nebraska Tractor Tests. This U is owned by Alan Draper of Bishopstone, Salisbury, Great Britain.

ABOVE: 1941 ALLIS-CHALMERS WF
This WF has the original A-C canopy. Approximately 8,000 Model WF standard-tread tractors were produced from 1937 to 1951 with steel wheels or rubber tires. The WF has the 29.93 belt horsepower gasoline engine of 201-ci displacement.

BELOW: ALLIS-CHALMERS D19
The Allis-Chalmers D19 was only built for three years, from 1961 to 1963. A number of D19 variations were available, including gasoline, LP-gas, or diesel models as well as an industrial version painted in utility yellow. This D19, bearing serial number 13149, was built in 1963 and is from the Larry and Edwin Karg collection.

ALLIS-CHALMERS WD45

The WD45 diesel was introduced in 1955 with a six-cylinder 230-ci engine rated at a brawny 40 brake horsepower. A gasoline version used a 4-cylinder, 226-ci engine. The WD45 diesel created its power via an engine based on the great Buda diesels (Allis-Chalmers had bought out the Buda Company in the early 1950s to gain this expertise). This 1956 WD45, owned by Theodore Buisker of Davis, Illinois, is still used every day for farming. Buisker first drove a WD45 at the tender age of five years.

Chapter 7

Ford Tractors
The Ford Tractor with the Ferguson System

Henry Ford was born on a farm, and when he set out to build a farm tractor, his goal was to ease the workload on the back of the nation's farmers by building a tractor comparable in simplicity and low cost to his Model T automobile .

Ford's first tractor experiments were based on Ford car chassis, which was not surprising as numerous other firms were offering kits to convert Model T cars into crude but effective farm tractors. In 1907, Ford unveiled his Automobile Plow based on a Model B car engine, but it remained a prototype until the famous—and infamous—Fordson tractor made its debut in 1917.

The Fordson earned praise and curses as one of the pioneer general-purpose tractors. With increased competition from International Harvester's Farmall, the Fordson ceased production in the United States in 1928, although they continued manufacturing in Dagenham, England.

In 1939, Ford re-entered the tractor market with the Ford 9N, which was supplemented by the three-point hitch and draft control features created by Harry Ferguson. Ford's N Series of tractors were revolutionary for the time, continuing in production until the handshake agreement between Ford Motor Company and Ferguson went sour in the 1940s.

ON PAGE 64: FORDSON MODEL F

The F had a 251-ci L-head four-cylinder engine rated at 10 drawbar horsepower and 20 horsepower on the belt. From early 1918 to 1928 nearly 850,000 Fordsons were manufactured. In 1925 almost 75 percent of the world's tractors were Fordsons. Owner—Palmer Fossum.

ABOVE: FORD 9N WITH FERGUSON SYSTEM

This Ford-Ferguson 9N tractor, serial number 357, is believed to be one of the oldest surviving 9Ns. Possibly built during the first week of production in 1939, it bears several imprints of the earliest N Series tractors. Note the horizontal grille and the early cast-aluminum hood; later 9Ns had vertical grilles and steel hoods. This tractor was restored by Ford collector Palmer Fossum of Northfield, Minnesota.

LEFT: FORD 9N WITH FERGUSON SYSTEM

The four-cylinder 120-ci L-head Ford engine produced 28 horsepower at 2,000 rpm. The success of the 9N was due to its low price and the Ferguson System created by Irishman Harry Ferguson. The system's innovative, yet brilliantly simple, three-point hitch and draft control revolutionized farm tractors.

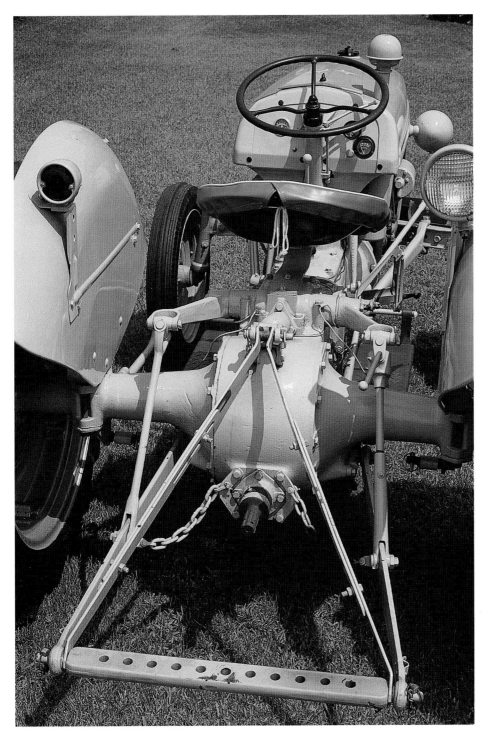

FORD 2N WITH FERGUSON SYSTEM

The Ford 2N replaced the original 1939 9N in 1942, hence its "2" designation just as the earlier tractor bore the 9. From this view, the famous Ferguson System three-point hitch is clearly visible. Using hydraulic touch controls, a farmer could attach or detach implements without straining a muscle or wasting time. This 1946 2N is owned by Leroy Folkert.

ABOVE: 1958 FORD 800 SERIES POWERMASTER 861
The 861 was built from 1958 to 1961, with a choice of diesel, LPG, and gasoline engines. This 861 has the four-cylinder 172-ci gasoline engine. Owner—Floyd Dominique.

RIGHT: FORD 501 OFFSET WORKMASTER
The Ford Motor Company and Harry Ferguson parted ways after a falling out over the handshake agreement between Ferguson and Henry Ford. Ferguson began building his own Ferguson tractors while Ford started its own line, including this 1958 501 Offset Workmaster. Designed for underframe-mounted tillage of sugar cane and vineyard farms, the 501 was powered by a four-cylinder 134-ci Red Tiger engine with a four-speed gearbox. This 501 was restored and is owned by Palmer Fossum of Northfield, Minnesota.

Chapter 8

Oliver and Hart Parr Tractors
The Company That Coined the Word "Tractor"

In 1897, Charles Hart and Charles Parr of Iowa combined forces to create the Hart-Parr Gasoline Engine Company in Madison, Wisconsin, although it soon moved to Charles City, Iowa. Hart-Parr built its first tractor in 1901 and coined the word *tractor* in 1906 to describe its self-propelled gasoline traction engine. The company continued to produce some of the nation's largest and most powerful tractors through the early parts of the twentieth century.

In 1929, Hart-Parr merged with the Oliver Chilled Plow Company of South Bend, Indiana; Nichols & Shepard Company of Battle Creek, Michigan; and the American Seeding Machine Company of Springfield, Ohio, to become the Oliver Farm Equipment Company.

With this merger, the new firm offered a full line of tractors, tillage tools, and farm implements to battle the main marketplace forces of Deere and Company and International Harvester. In 1937 Hart-Parr was dropped from the nameplate.

Together with Minneapolis-Moline and Cockshutt Plow Company of Brantford, Ontario (which sold Oliver tractors under its own name), Oliver became part of the White Motor Corporation in 1962.

ON PAGE 70: OLIVER 880

The successor to the Super 88, the 880 had Power-Booster drive, Power-Traction hitch, and power adjusted rear wheel spacing. The 265-ci six-cylinder engine was available with the usual three types of fuel options: diesel, gasoline, and LPG. Production ran from 1958 to 1962.

RIGHT: HART-PARR 12-24

In 1901, Charles Hart and Charles Parr joined forces to produce the stalwart Hart-Parr tractor series, finding a home in Charles City, Iowa. In 1929, Hart-Parr merged with the Oliver Chilled Plow Company and other firms, becoming the Oliver Corporation. Hart-Parr's 12-24 was a successful twin-cylinder tractor rated at 12 drawbar horsepower and 24 belt-pulley horsepower.

LEFT: OLIVER ROW CROP

The Oliver 18-27 row-crop used the same engine and transmission as the standard-tread 18-28. Built between 1931 and 1937, it was the forerunner of the Oliver 80.

ABOVE: OLIVER ROW CROP 77

In 1948, Oliver introduced its Fleetline Series of tractors with modern styling and streamlined, enclosed engines. The Row Crop 66, 77, and 88 models replaced the old 60, 70, and 80 models, respectively, and were built until 1954. This powerful, smooth, six-cylinder, 40-horsepower Row Crop 77 was typical of the new fleetlines, and boasted the new Hydra-Lectric hydraulics system beginning in 1949.

NEXT PAGE: 1955 OLIVER 99 DIESEL

This six-cylinder diesel with a 302-ci displacement has a bore and stroke of 4 inches and a 15.5:1 compression ratio. This rare tractor is owned by Charlie Lulich of Mason, Wisconsin.

ABOVE: 1920 HART-PARR 30 MODEL A
This has the two-cylinder, side-by-side horizontal engine with a large 6.50x7.00 inch bore and stroke. The transmission had only two forward speeds, giving 1.98 miles per hour and a top gear speed of 2.88 miles per hour. The Model 30 was rated at 30 belt horsepower and 15 at the drawbar. Owner David Preuhs, Minnesota.

LEFT: 1936 OLIVER HART-PARR 28-44
The 28-24 was a development of the Model A, which evolved into the 90 and then the 99 Oliver. The big four- to five-plow tractor used the four-cylinder, overhead-valve 443-ci kerosene engine, with a bore and stroke of 4.75x6.25 inches. The transmission has three forward gears.

Chapter 9

The Orphan Tractors
Tractors of Many Colors

Tractor historians have traced the lineage of more than 1,000 different American and Canadian tractor manufacturers that built at least one model.

Many of these manufacturers were blacksmiths who created a one-off tractor or small ventures that built a prototype that never made it into series production. Others built a range of models over several decades before being chased out of business by the giant corporations.

These once-upon-a-time tractor makers are collectively known as the orphan brands.

Among the numerous brands of orphan tractors were many creative, even revolutionary, ideas—as well as just oddball inventions. Consider the Hackney Auto Plow, made in St. Paul, Minnesota, in the 1910s, which was basically an automobile fitted with an undercarriage plow. Or the Chase Motor Truck from Syracuse, New York, which ran on three rolling drums and was termed a tractor-roller.

And there was also the Happy Farmer tractor from Minneapolis, the crawler Auto-Track-Tractor from San Francisco, designed to run in the moist soil of the California valleys, and many more. The history of these orphan tractors was as varied as the colors they were painted.

ON PAGE 80: 1954 Cockshutt D-50 Diesel

Using a six-cylinder, 273-ci Buda diesel engine, this tractor produced 53 PTO horsepower and 47 horsepower at the drawbar. Manufactured from 1953 to 1957, this Model 50 was also sold as the Co-Op E5. Owner—Jim Grant.

ABOVE: FARM MOTORS TILSOIL 18-30

The Farm Motors Company of Canada built its massive Tilsoil 18-30 tractor in 1922. The engine had a 7.00x8.00 inch bore and stroke and reached a maximum engine operating speed of 700 rpm, enough to push the Tilsoil to a 3.25-mile-per-hour top speed. Only about 300 of these monstrous 6,300-pound tractors were ever built.

RIGHT: ROBERT BELL IMPERIAL SUPER-DRIVE

The famous Canadian Robert Bell Engine & Thresher Company of Seaforth, Ontario, was a successful builder of a range of threshing machines. Robert Bell also sold a line of farm tractors in the 1920s, including this Imperial Super-Drive. The Imperial was actually built by the Illinois Tractor Company of Bloomington, Illinois, and sold under Bell's name in Canada. This Imperial Super-Drive was photographed at the Ontario Agricultural Museum show at the Great Canadian Field Days in Milton, Ontario.

ABOVE: GRAY-DORT

This 1920 Gray-Dort was built as a joint venture by Gray Sons–Campbell of Chatham, Canada, and the Dort Motor Company of Detroit. Interesting features are the 20-inch truck rims on mower wheels and the Chevrolet steering. This rare bit of history is owned by Rick Guy of Ontario, Canada.

LEFT: GRAY-DORT

The Gray-Dort was not an actual farm tractor but a converted automobile, a popular modification with down-and-out farmers during the Great Depression of the 1930s.

SAMSON MODEL M

A 2x14-inch bottom-plow tractor, the M was General Motors' answer to the Fordson Model F. General Motors President W. C. Durant was worried that arch-rival Ford was going to build tractors, therefore in 1917 he acquired the Samson Company, builders of the Sieve-Grip tractor. General Motors soon designed a more conventional tractor, the Model M, with the 276-ci four-cylinder Northway motor. This was very similar to the Ford engine in size. However, in 1922 the Samson Tractor Division was shut down by General Motors for being unprofitable.

ABOVE: DUPLEX CO-OP NO. 2
The top-of-the-range Co-op No. 2 was powered by the smooth, powerful six-cylinder Chrysler engine, which gave a reputed top speed of 28 miles per hour. This rare tractor is owned by Ivan Henderson of Hutchinson, Ontario, Canada.

LEFT: DUPLEX CO-OP NO. 2
The Duplex Machinery Company of Battle Creek, Michigan, introduced its No. 1 tractor in 1937. The No. 1 was followed by the No. 2; this No. 2 was built in 1938 and bears serial number 1165. In mid-1938, Duplex Machinery changed its name to the Co-operative Manufacturing Company.

AVERY RO-TRACK

The Avery Farm Equipment Company built the Ro-Track in Peoria, Illinois, in 1938. The complex, soft-sprung, adjustable front axle was convertible from a narrow to a wide track. Powered by the 212-ci, L-head, six-cylinder, gasoline Hercules engine with a three-speed transmission, it was rated as a two- to three-plow tractor. The Avery Company started in 1874 with steam traction engines and then went into gasoline tractors with some successful models. However, the company struggled through the Great Depression until closure in 1941.

ABOVE: FRIDAY MODEL 048
The Friday Tractor Company of Hartford, Michigan, first offered its Model 048 in about 1948. The Friday was designed specifically for orchard use and for delivering produce to market. The Friday line was offered into the late 1950s.

LEFT: 1938 GRAHAM-BRADLEY
This 32-horsepower tractor was powered by the six-cylinder Graham Paige engine with a 3.25x4.75 inch bore and stroke. This long-stroke engine gave a 20-mile-per-hour top speed. Car builder Graham-Paige Motors Corporation of Detroit, Michigan, produced this row-crop model in 1938, followed by the 104 model in 1939. This was the same tractor but had standard tread. Production ceased in 1945.

BELOW: FRIDAY MODEL 048
This 1949 Model 048 had a six-cylinder, Chrysler Industrial, 90-horsepower engine backed by a Dodge five-speed gearbox and a two-speed rear axle. Top speed was about 60 miles per hour, making the Friday ideal for hauling produce to market. This Friday Model 048 is owned by Larry Darling of Hartford, Michigan, where the tractors were once built.

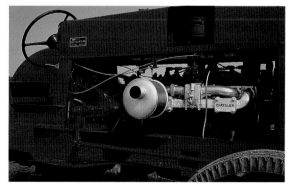

WATERLOO BRONCO

The Waterloo Company of Ontario, Canada, offered its Bronco row-crop tractor between the years 1948 and 1950, though only about 1,000 were ever built. This firm is not to be confused with other tractor makes using the name Waterloo in their titles, including the Waterloo Gasoline Engine Company of Waterloo, Iowa, builders of the famous Waterloo Boy.

Index

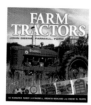

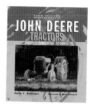

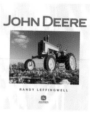

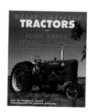